EST. 2013

COTTON + STEEL

AUTHENTIC

COLORING BOOK

75+ WHIMSICAL DESIGNS TO COLOR AND LOVE

Fons&Porter
CINCINNATI, OHIO

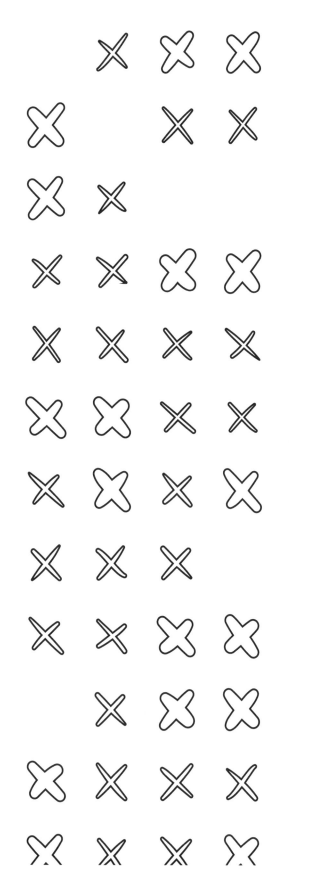

INTRODUCTION

Do you remember when you were a kid, sitting at the table with your siblings or cousins, doodling away in a coloring book? What about making macaroni necklaces or playing with clay? Cotton+Steel is all about that same creative camaraderie. Our five designers are unusually collaborative. We share our sketches and ideas with each other, give each other feedback, and sometimes even build on each other's artwork. The best part is when our customers start the process all over again by choosing Cotton+Steel fabrics as the building blocks to make something uniquely their own.

We are delighted to be a part of such a fun, imaginative industry, and now, with this coloring book, you can join in our creative process by lending your own sense of color to every page. We've included art from all five of our designers, sometimes mixing and matching our designs into a single page. We have a little of everything here; Rashida's Japanese-inspired motifs, Melody's vintage telephones and typewriters, Alexia's hand-painted tigers, Sarah's horses and bunnies, and Kim's delightful feedsack prints all make an appearance. Can you guess which designs belong to which designer?

We welcome you into our world of art, whimsy, and wonder. Start with our designs, and make them your own. Here's your chance to be the designer and finish the art your way.

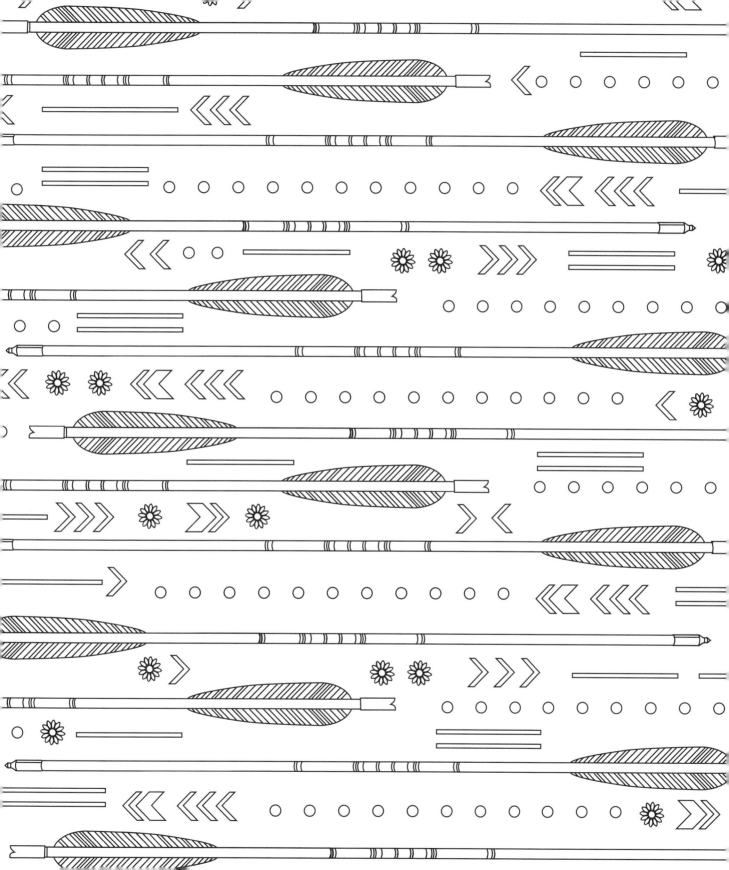

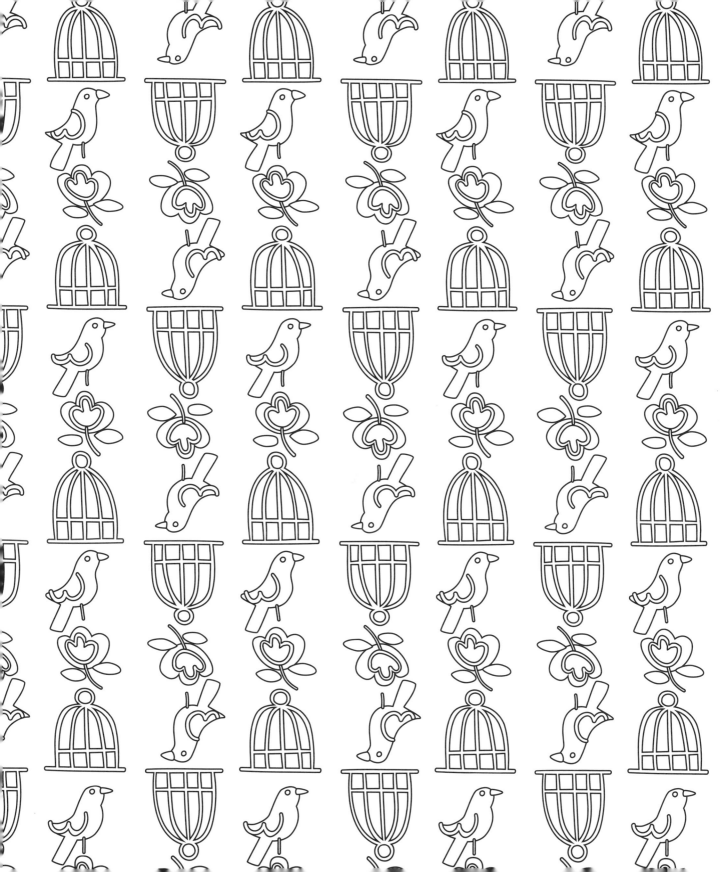

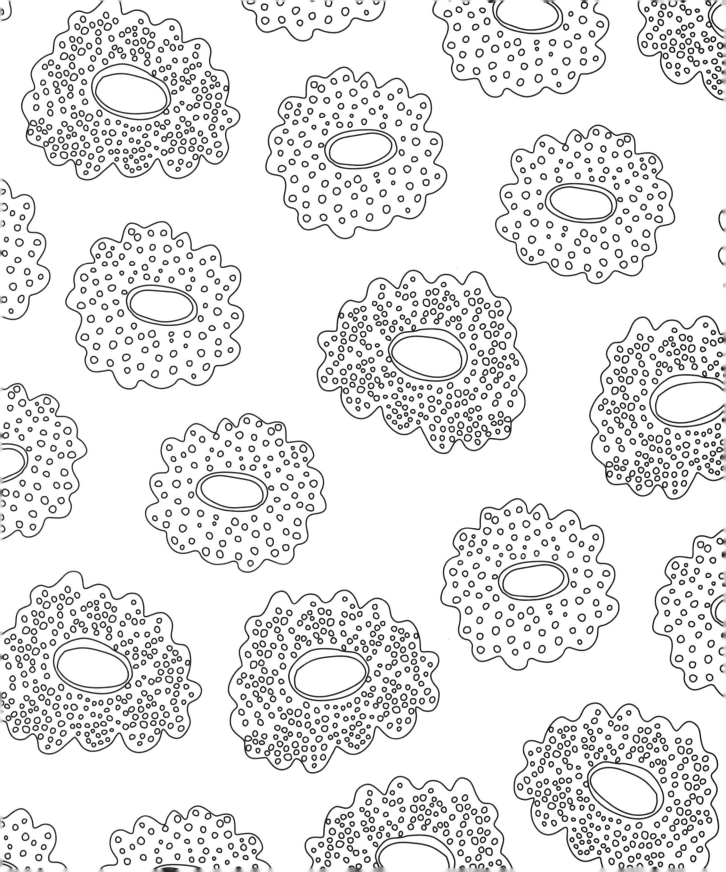

HOLLYWOOD

NASHVILLE

SAN FRANCISCO

PARIS

DRAW YOUR OWN!

TOKYO

NEW YORK CITY

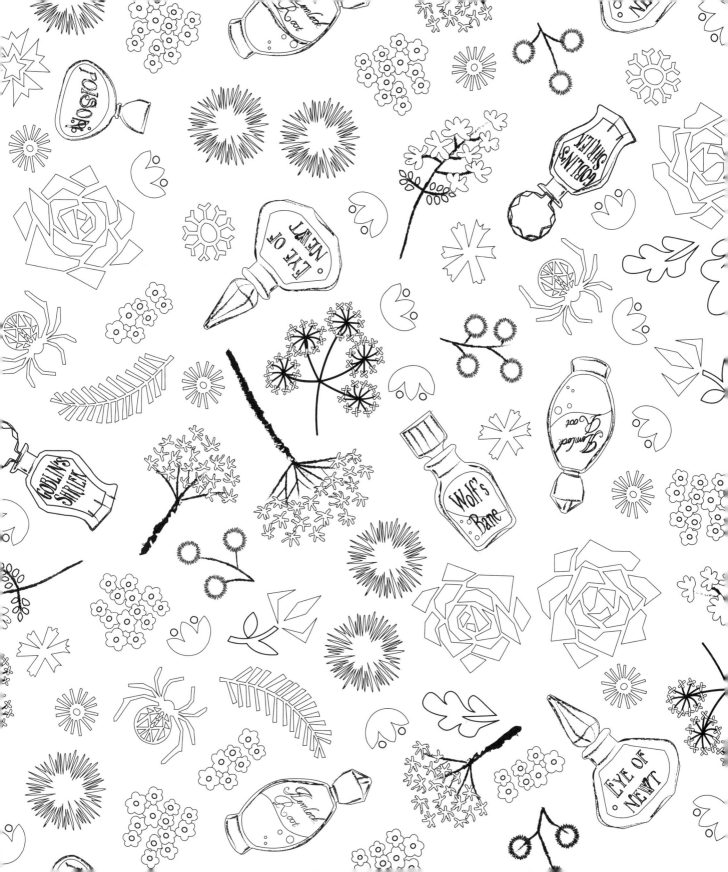

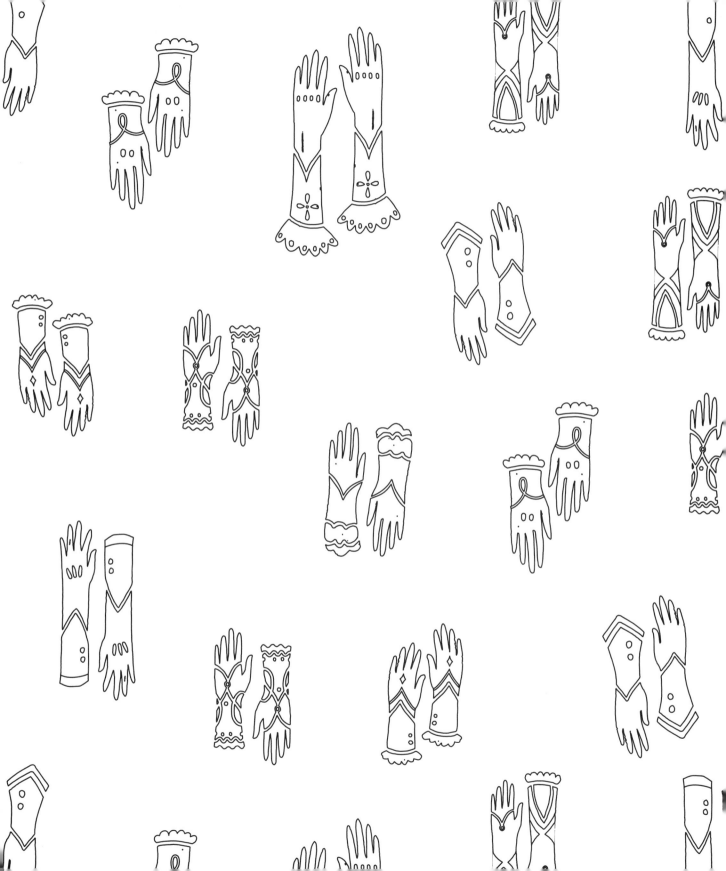

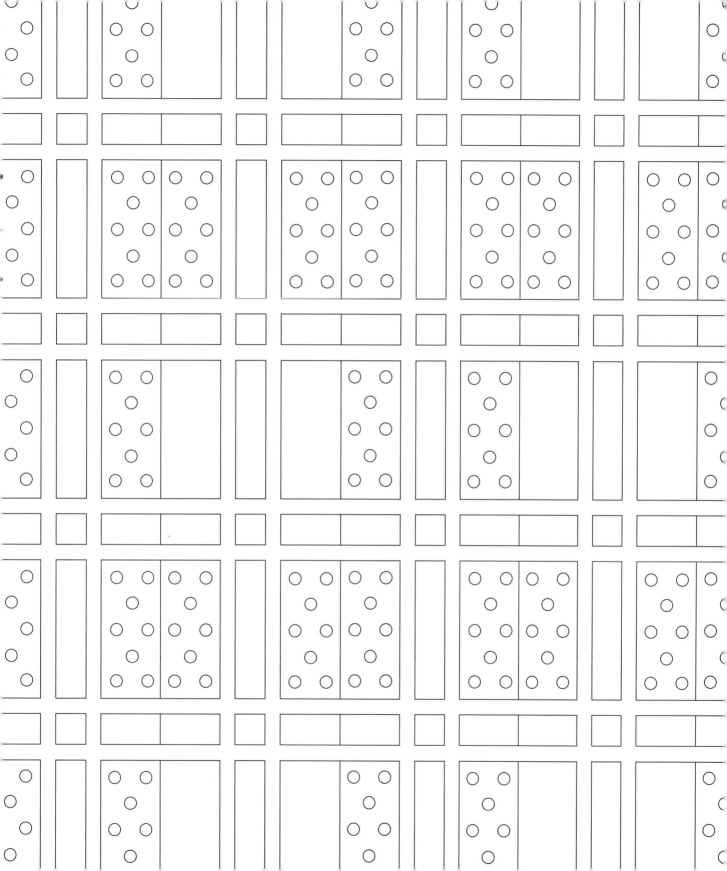

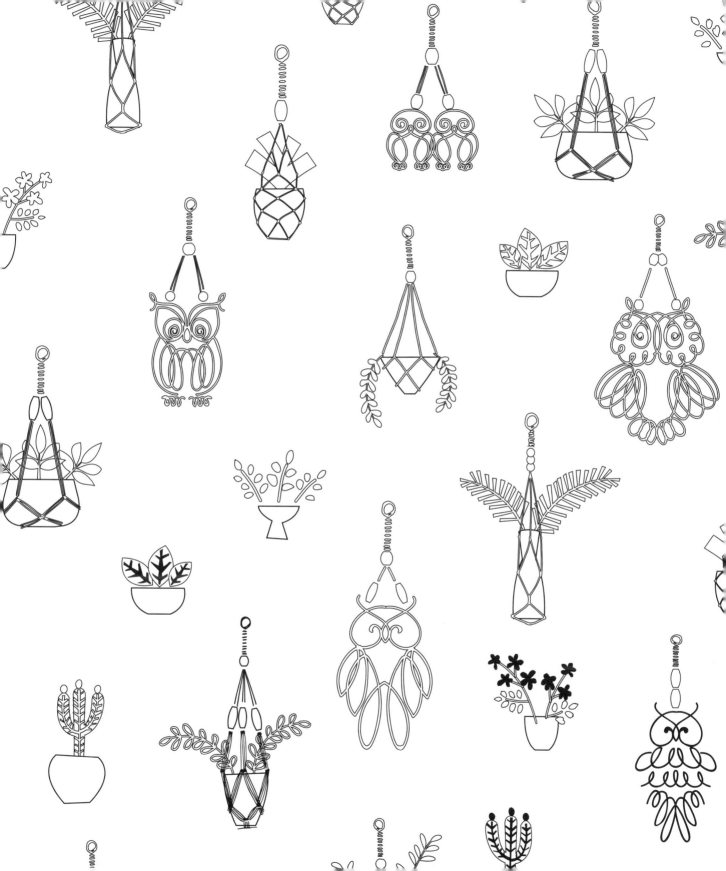

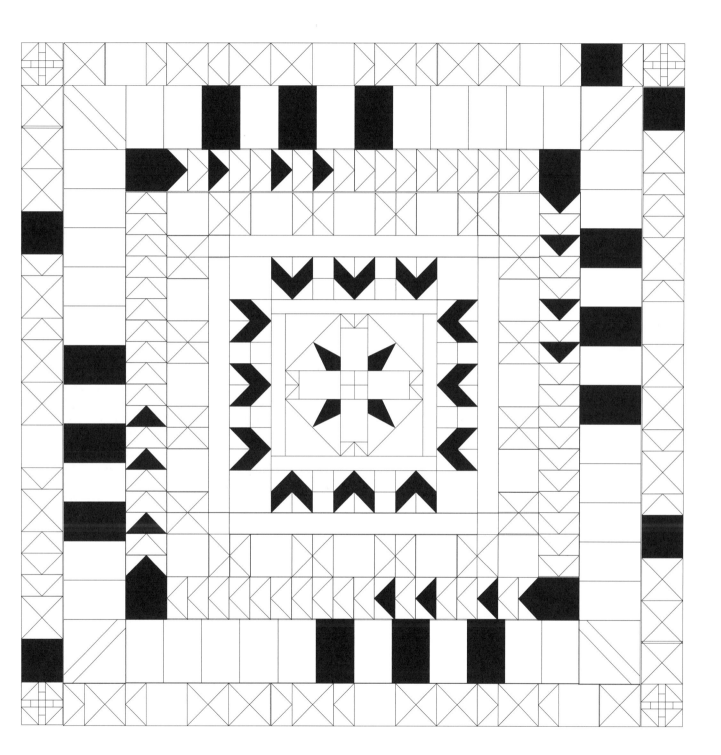

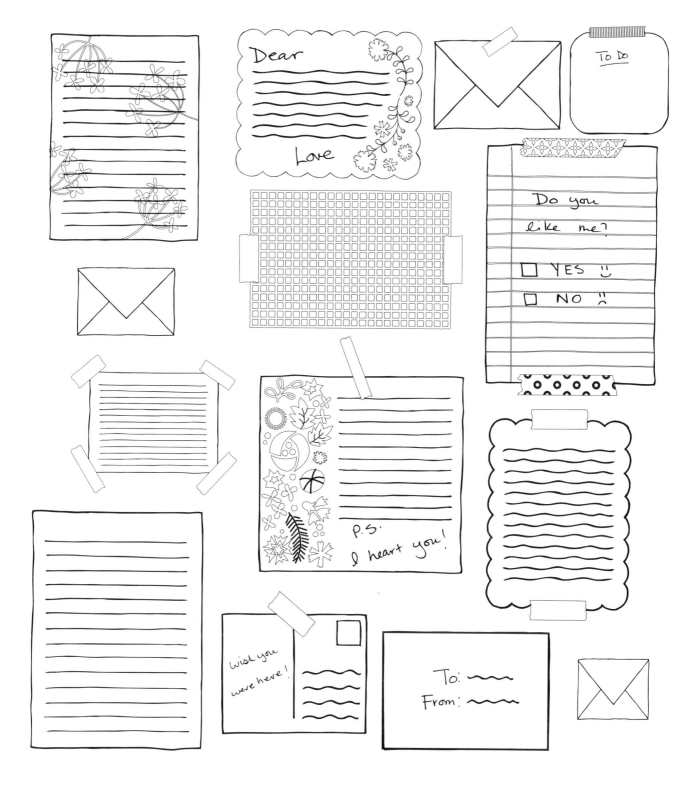

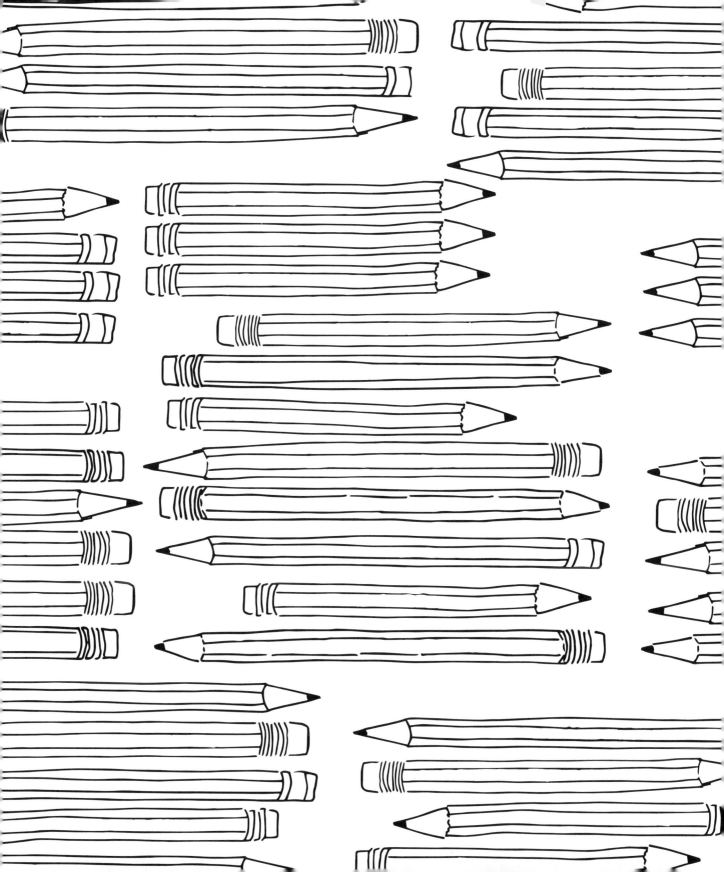

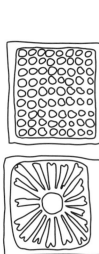

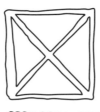

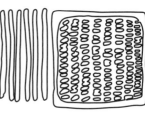

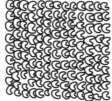
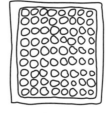

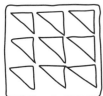

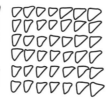

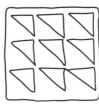

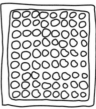

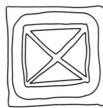
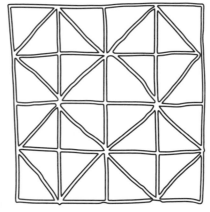

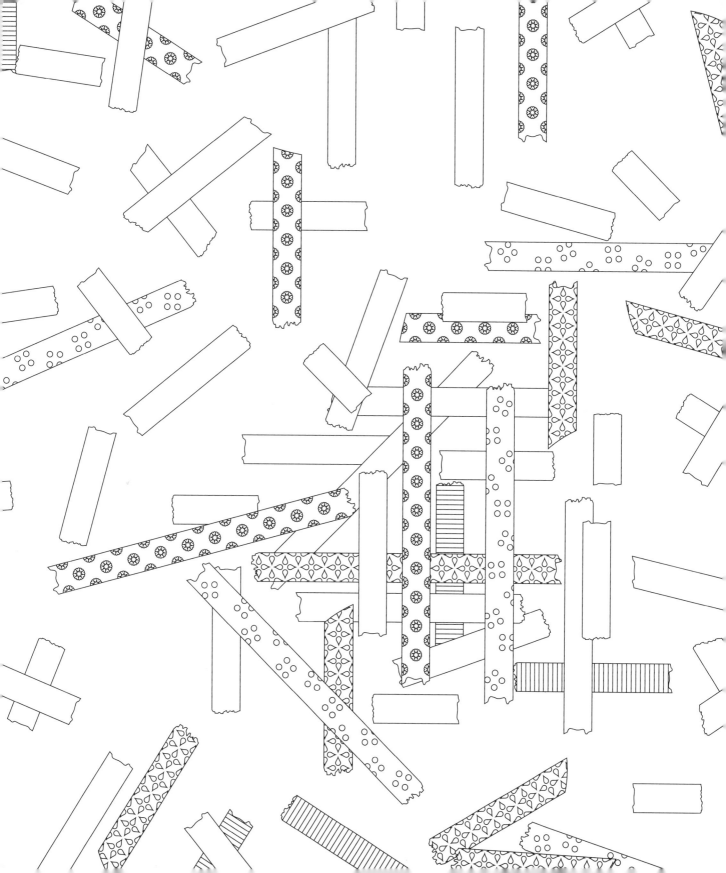

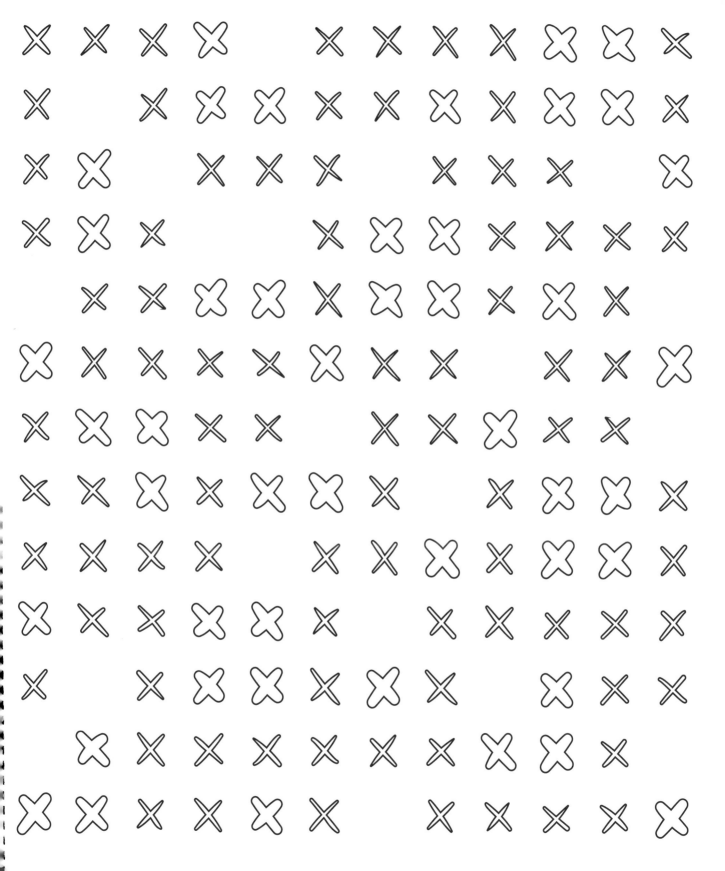

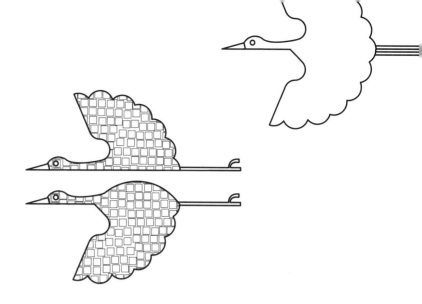

ABOUT COTTON+STEEL

As a young company, Cotton+Steel hopes to honor the traditions of creativity, resourcefulness, and innovation inherent in the sewing and quilting world. The five designers Melody Miller, Sarah Watts, Rashida Coleman-Hale, Alexia Marcelle Abegg, and Kimberly Kight are unusually collaborative, and their fabrics can be found in shops across the world. The designs in this book reflect the designers' personal aesthetic and their collaborative spirit.

Melody Miller - Creative Director, Founding Designer

Melody grew up in the Lowcountry of South Carolina, quite possibly the prettiest place on earth. Later, she felt just as much at home in New York City, where she studied industrial design at Pratt Institute, and her love for vintage objects began. She is the designer behind the Ruby Star fabric lines for Kokka, as well as co-author of the book, *Ruby Star Wrapping*. In early 2013, Melody had an epic idea, and from that, Cotton+Steel was born. She lives in Atlanta, in picturesque and historic Grant Park, with her amazing photographer hubby, two charmingly quirky children, and a very silly Bichon Frise. She loves vintage design, flea markets, her converse sneaks and margaritas. Most times, in moderation.

Sarah Watts - Founding Designer

Sarah Watts is a fabric designer, book illustrator, and licensing artist based in Atlanta, Georgia. After a nomadic childhood filled with characters and interesting narratives, she studied at Ringling College of Art and Design, and put her imagination to great use as an illustrator. Sarah has previously designed for Blend Fabrics; Timber and Leaf was her most notable collection. In addition to designing fabric, Sarah has a full line of aprons and kitchen towels, and licenses her art to other products as well. She has also illustrated several YA and children's books. Sarah's most recent adventures include skydiving, tattoos, and eloping in Vegas. Sewing has always been her favorite peaceful activity away from her sketchpad and computer. When she is not drawing or sewing, she likes going thrifting and adventuring in nature with her awesome husband. Sarah finds bliss in the smell of a campfire and a good cup of black coffee.

Rashida Coleman-Hale - Founding Designer

Rashida Coleman-Hale has been making things ever since she can remember. She studied fashion design at the Fashion Institute of Technology in New York City. Not sure if fashion was her calling, she traded her sewing machine for a computer and worked as a freelance graphic designer. Her passion for sewing was rekindled in 2006 after the arrival of her first child, and she began the blog, I Heart Linen, to document her re-born creative life and her life as a stay-at-home mommy. A fabric designer as well as an author, Rashida has designed fabric for Timeless Treasures and Cloud 9 Fabrics. Her first book, *I Love Patchwork*, was published by Interweave press in Fall 2009 and was awarded the 2010 PubWest Book Design Bronze Medal in the How-To/Crafts category. Her second book, *Zakka Style*, was published by C&T Publishing in Fall 2011. Rashida lives in Atlanta with her husband and their three children.

Alexia Marcelle Abegg - Founding Designer

Alexia Marcelle Abegg was born in Folsom, California, on the day Mount St. Helens erupted. She has been inspired by her parents' creativity and dedication to art throughout her life. An award-winning designer, artist, and writer, Alexia has always been fascinated with the art of sewing. She studied fashion and fine arts in college. After trying her hand at photography, production, acting, costuming, hair and makeup for film and television, fashion design, and custom sewing, she found her home in creating fine art quilts and sewing patterns while living in Brooklyn, New York. Alexia and her husband, artist and fabric designer, Rob Bancroft, live in Nashville with their two dogs. She currently divides her time among creating patterns for their company—Green Bee Design and Patterns—teaching, making art and writing.

Kim Kight - Founding Designer

Kimberly Kight spent a lot of time as a child at the heels of her mom and grandma, shopping for fabric in the aisles of JC Penny and the like. Though she doesn't remember sewing on her own as a child, when she received a sewing machine as a gift in 2001, she was able to thread it without thinking about it. A layoff led to a sewing hobby that led to an interest in fabric. She started the blog, True Up, in 2008 as a new era of fabric design was beginning to emerge. In 2011, her first book, *A Field Guide to Fabric Design*, was published. An avid collector of vintage fabric, she wants to bring her very favorite prints from the past back for a new generation of sewers to enjoy. Kim lives in the Hill Country just outside of Austin, Texas with her husband and two sons.

fw

a content + ecommerce company

19 18 17 16   5 4 3 2

Distributed in Canada by Fraser Direct
100 Armstrong Avenue
Georgetown, ON, Canada L7G 5S4
Tel: (905) 877-4411

Distributed in the U.K. and Europe by F&W MEDIA INTERNATIONAL
Brunel House, Newton Abbot, Devon, TQ12 4PU, England
Tel: (+44) 1626 323200, Fax: (+44) 1626 323319
E-mail: enquiries@fwmedia.com

Distributed in Australia by Capricorn Link
P.O. Box 704, S. Windsor NSW, 2756 Australia
Tel: (02) 4560 1600, Fax: (02) 4577 5288
E-mail: books@capricornlink.com.au

SRN: S8736
ISBN-13: 978-1-4402-4630-2

Edited by Amelia Johanson
Designed by Michelle Roy Kelly
Production coordinated by Jennifer Bass
Illustrations by the Designers of Cotton + Steel